Born To (W)alk (i)n (N)ewness (WIN)

the journey of overcoming depression, a miscarriage, homelessness, unemployment, and divorce to find love, joy, peace, and wholeness

Bronda Bessant

Copyright © 2021 by Bronda Bessant

All Rights Reserved. No part of this publication may be reproduced, distributed, or transmitted in any form or by any means, including photocopying, recording, or other electronic or mechanical methods, without the prior written permission of the publisher, except in the case of brief quotations embodied in critical reviews and certain other noncommercial uses permitted by copyright law. For permission requests, contact the author at uniqueindividual8521@gmail.com.

ISBN: 978-1-955572-01-9
Library of Congress Cataloging-in-Publication Data
Library of Congress Control Number:

Printed in the United States of America
First printing edition 2021.

Cover design by Shuvodsgner
Edited by Jerra Latrice at Gifted With a Pen

This is a work of nonfiction. No names have been changed, no characters invented, no events fabricated. Although the author and publisher have made every effort to ensure that the information in this book was correct at press time, the author and publisher do not assume and hereby disclaim any liability to any party for any loss, damage, or disruption caused by errors or omissions, whether such errors or omissions result from negligence, accident, or any other cause.

Table of Contents

Dedication v

Acknowledgments vi

Introduction vii

Chapter 1: Born to (W)alk (i)n (N)ewness (WIN) 1

Chapter 2: I Couldn't Hear 3

Chapter 3: Birthed in My Pain 7

Chapter 4: I Never Knew Love 11

Chapter 5: The Reflection in the Mirror Runs Deep 13

Chapter 6: They Needed Saving from Me 15

Chapter 7: Changing My Heart Changed My Life 19

Chapter 8: Encouraging Others Needing Encouragement Myself 23

Chapter 9: You Know My Name, You Don't Know My Story ... 27

Chapter 10: Accepting Being Set Apart 31

Chapter 11: Unique Individual 33

Chapter 12: Footprints to finding my Identity 35

Chapter 13: Mother under God's Dominion 37

Chapter 14: Not About that Life 39

Chapter 15: Pushing Thru Darkness into the Light 43

Chapter 16: My Love Has Conditions 45

Chapter 17: A Long Road to Finding a Place to Call Home 49

Chapter 18: Cut from a Different Cloth 59

Chapter 19: To My Black Man 65

Chapter 20: Don't Chase After a Man 69

Chapter 21: I Don't Care What People Say 71

Chapter 22: This is Who God Made Me 75

About the Author 79

DEDICATION

To my three beloved beautiful daughters who are greater than I - My Sunshine, Ms. Love, and MaMa Girl - I love each of you from life to infinity. I am beyond proud of the women on the grow you are. Thank you is not enough to each of you for enduring my brokenness to find wholesomeness of loving myself, and finding joy and peace. Love and light always. Love you each much!!

ACKNOWLEDGMENTS

First and foremost, I want to thank God, my Creator, Lord and Savior, My Everything for His unwavering love, kindness, faithfulness, grace, mercy, and patience for and towards me. I never would have made it without Him. To my father, mother, sister, and brother, thank you for loving me as I was growing to be a loving, wiser, stronger, and better me.

Introduction

Born to Walk in Newness is a compilation of written works chronicled about my life's journey and experiences, as it is thus far, by way of the Holy Spirit. On my own, I could have never written or come up with these thoughts. There were times like now and a period from February 5, 2018 until late 2019, when I was battling a concussion, which led to post-concussion syndrome.

During these times, like now, my thoughts were scattered, I struggled to communicate verbally, as my thoughts were all over the place, and I suffered headaches, anxiety, irritability, confusion, loss of concentration, and memory. I am struggling and have been since January 28, 2021, when I was injured in the line of duty. I do my best to try to read to understand because I don't want to lose my mind. Honestly, it is scary not being able to get my thoughts together.

But, by the grace of God, He keeps on keeping me, in spite of what I am enduring and experiencing emotionally, mentally, and physically. So, I am ever so grateful for His love, faithfulness, kindness, and patience towards and for me. This is the only thing that keeps and has kept me going. There are days when and where I have been in excruciating pain physically. Yet, with each God given day, I am able to do for and take care of myself, and I have no complaints.

I know someone somewhere is at the mercy of someone else, waiting on them to come see about them. Yes, life has dealt me some cards of pain. Thankfully, in and by God's grace, I am good!! I can remember before 2005, I was praying and worrying. But, after the first time, the death angel came to take my life, when I had my miscarriage, my life changed. As I was walking out the door, the Holy Spirit said to me, "When you return you won't be the same." And, I have not been the same since that time.

I no longer fear death. I am not afraid of dying today if God saw to take me. On the other hand, I am afraid to live or step outside of His will for my life. No, I am not perfect, I don't choose to be, could never be, and don't want to be. However, I do my best to do everything I do with excellence. In addition to this, I live my life according to the Bible and principles of Christ.

God has also given and equipped me with a tenacity of strength, perseverance, resilience, and fortitude beyond my comprehensibility. Truly, beyond grateful and indebted to Him with my life. This is where *Born to Walk in Newness* was born.

In order to rewrite the trajectory of one's story, they must reinvent themselves moving from brokenness to wholeness. This is and will be null and void if we don't address the cards we hold in our hands by letting go the pain of our past. The pain of our past buries the pain and cries of our inner child.

The pain rages, roars, and radiates in the display of our heart's cry driving our emotions, behaviors, and thoughts manifesting and reflecting hidden motives and agendas. Hence, as hard as it is to confront our internal demons, it is even harder existing alive while dying, when we can live and thrive becoming our best selves. For some of us, healing requires seeking and getting professional help with getting wholesome and healthy.

In order to live conquering, persevering, and thriving beyond the pain and hurt of our yesterday requires looking in the mirror, reflecting to the soul of your root to address and kill the fruit of our hurt and pain, to come no more or rise again. Healing requires intentionality of putting in the necessary work to your healing.

Reflections of my journey from brokenness, hurt, and pain rising to the wholeness of being Born to (W)alk (i)n (N)ewness (WIN).

Chapter 1

Born to (W)alk (I)n (N)ewness (WIN)

Each and everyone of us has a story. A beginning we cannot change, a middle to accept, embrace, acknowledge, and let go, and an end to walking in the newness of who Christ says we are. We are not what we have done, been through, n'or endured. Everyone has a known name, a story we lived, don't know, and will discover. A truth of mercy and grace to share.

Everyone's story is an unwritten book. On the other hand, not everyone will write, tell, or share their truth. God is no respective person; what He's done for me, He will also do for you. Your past does not determine your future. Your strength, determination, and will to succeed walking your God given identity does.

Ask me, *how do I know?* I was Born to Walk in Newness, and so are you. You only fail out of your fear to get up after a fall. I have fallen and failed many times at many things. I got up in God's grace, and you can too. Put your faith in action and your hand to the plow of redeeming yourself. In Christ, all things are possible if you put in the work required and believe in yourself, even if and when no one else does.

Honestly, the way my life is set up, it has been nothing but pain on top of pain, one thing after another. Lord, will you please give me a break. Each test, trial, and tribulation strengthened my faith muscle, which was being stretched to totally trusting God, with every fiber of my being. I had no one to call or turn to, but Him.

I prayed, picked up my Bible and searched out His affirming steadfast righteous word. It is here I found strength to persevere, stand, endure, withstand, and conquer every test, trials, and tribulation that came my way. There is no way I would have made it had I not had unwavering unshakable faith, trust, and belief in God.

Chapter 2

I Couldn't Hear

The words, *"For most of my life,"* resound so loudly throughout the premise of the majority of my life. Surely, I listened to respond and not to hear. Sometimes, I was totally zoned out. It's especially hard for me to listen to someone who will not take ownership of their own stuff, by continuously avoiding to take responsibility for their actions. However, checking out on such a person is a missed opportunity to be fully present with the person on their way to healing.

Oftentimes, I found myself interjecting while the person was speaking. But, overtime I got better. The reason for my lack of hearing is because I felt that I was never listened to, heard, or understood. As a child, I was also acting out to get attention. Growing into an adult, I never took the time out to understand the root of my hearing deficit, or how I arrived at this place. Once again,

Born To (W)alk (i)n (N)ewness (WIN)

I had to address my inner child in order to heal as an adult.

What I realized is that I had to look back in my life to acknowledge, address, and confront my hurts, aches, and pain in order to get better. I also own and take responsibility for my shortcomings. There was no way to possibly get better without me accepting that I had an issue of concern. It was problematic and detrimental to my being, if I didn't come to the place where I became an effective listener who sought to understand, instead of responding.

The perfected art of listening to hear to understand, and not responding allows the listener to have an extension of safety and empathy leading to trust. When someone feels heard, it becomes a relationship bridging a gateway to emotional safety. When we truly seek to understand a person, we will be intentional about our ability to (h)elping (e)ncourage (a)ffirming (r)eflections (hear) others'.

I found that in order for me to be an effective counselor, I am first required to seek and get counseling, for myself. There was no way possible for me to be a counselor, if I had a deeply rooted bag of unaddressed baggage of triggers within the depths of my soul, waiting to erupt when I sat in the chair to hear and effectively listen to someone else's story. As long as I can't hear others, I am and will be ineffective in creating or being a helpful change agent to myself and others.

In essence, I seek to hear to understand my heart, first and foremost. The art of helping others starts and begins with me being healthy. I couldn't hear due to the clutter and chatter of my own unheard voice which was never understood. So, I began to talk too much, screaming to be heard; all the while, never listening to understand, but to respond.

I came across a caption with the words from Stephen Covey, "Most people do not listen with the intent to understand; they listen with the intent to reply." These words were like a quickening to me, as my middle daughter spoke them to me often. This was my confirming conviction I needed to address this area of my life. Hence, I am practicing being present, being quick to listen, and slow to speak (James 1:19).

Born To (W)alk (i)n (N)ewness (WIN)

CHAPTER 3

BIRTHED IN MY PAIN

For all of my life, I couldn't hear. I was allowed to do from a toddler to adulthood, to do whatever I wanted. I wasn't chastened, checked, or corrected when I had temper tantrums or fall outs. I was rolling my way into the highway of my youth, pre-teens, adolescence, and young adulthood; abusing myself, wandering aimlessly lost and unaware of my identity into womanhood.

Nevertheless, my saving grace was my grandmother's blessing of bestowing the gift of "Teach your children right from wrong, and when they are grown they will still do right," taken from Proverbs 22:6 (CEV). My grandmothers introduced me to Christ, as they knew Him and His word at an early age. Both my paternal and maternal grandmothers live and lived a life where their life's walk and witness aligned. They were servants to their own families extending and giving demonstrated love of service to their communities.

Unlike my parents, they were old-school. It is here with them I got chastened, checked, and corrected through their talking and sparing the rod of love. It is here that this book was birthed in my pain. While writing these reflections, this was the most challenging time I have ever faced in my life. After being exposed to COVID-19, I have experienced and suffered for an entire year up until this present time, still experiencing coughing, dizziness, shortness of breath, and chest pains.

Here is the thing - although I have never had a positive test or developed antibodies, I have experienced headaches, chills, nausea, diarrhea, sweats, vomiting, syncope, dizziness, shortness of breath, chest pains, body aches, chronic fatigue, and thrash. I have seen my primary care, infectious disease control, multiple pulmonologists , multiple ENTS, gastroenterologist, cardiologist- just a host of medical professionals. I would be considered one of the unheard long haulers without a positive COVID test.

To date, no one has been able to confirm indefinitely what's wrong with me. In July of 2020, as a result of this exposure, I developed pneumonia and was only breathing sixty percent at the time. TDJ, who I took to be a trusted friend, knew all of this. Initially, he was very supportive. This was his representative though.

Later, he showed his true self. Still, I have love for him and respect him from a distance. God used him to show me it is okay to let my guard down to my "(h)elping (i)nspire (m)arvelousness (him)."

" (H)elping (e)veryone (he)" just got a glimpse of my pure heart to serve. And, the others who know some of my story can better understand my struggling to getting and arriving at the place of understanding I was Born to (W)alk (i)n (N)ewness (WIN). This book was birthed in my pain. I couldn't have done this without God. He is "MY" source, resource, and belief rock of safety.

I am not infringing or putting my beliefs on anyone. This is my story, as you too have yours to be written in the truth of your voice and reality as well, if you feel deemed and compelled to do so. Never be afraid to accept, acknowledge, and embrace your truth by letting go and thriving in your new season. You too are Born to (W)alk (i)n (N)ewness (WIN).

Born To (W)alk (i)n (N)ewness (WIN)

CHAPTER 4

I NEVER KNEW LOVE

I never knew love because I was always giving myself away freely. My foundation of broken Ideology of a man laid out my blueprint of wanting, needing, and seeking a man's love. This was a result of my father being an absent male figure in my life. Although I have parents, I was not parented. I did not know what it was to have someone to be there to support, protect, correct, chasten, and cover me.

My father lived a life in the streets, instead of one spent honoring, loving, protecting, and providing for his family. As a result of this, I was always running him down for attention and attempting to get him to do right by himself and our family. He had gainful employment for the majority of my life, however, we lived in poverty because he wasted his time and money in the streets. There were times when we had little to no food and no lights. In addition, we did not have heat.

If it had not been for my mother, I do not know where I would be. I took myself through some hard knock lessons due to not having a man in my life to show me what it is to be loved, honored, or respected by a man. Not knowing love, I married a man who was just like my father. But, that was my blessing in disguise. It was here that I learned to love myself. After being in that abusive disrespectful relationship for seven years, when God blessed me to get free, I found me.

Henceforth, I never knew love died and was buried in July of 2013 when God granted me a divorce. My husband divorced me. Since then, I have not dated much. I took time to get to know me, and learned to allow a man to love and pursue me. In God's timing what will be, will be. Until then, The Lord is healing from my truth of never knowing love. *How can I experience and have what I have never known or had?*

First and foremost, I had to come to get to know and love myself. A place of not needing validation from others. On the other hand, I am comfortable with being and standing alone for what I believe in. However, I had to stop giving my best and treasured gifts of self and time away so freely to those who do not deserve neither.

Chapter 5

The Reflection in the Mirror Runs Deep

Boy, did I have to learn the hard way that my body is scared not meant to be shared until marriage! However, due to the cards of life I was dealt, I had to accept, learn from, and grow through the hard knock lessons of pain I endured. It took me a very long time to get it, but I got on the other side of Heaven. For this, I am extremely grateful to God.

Nonetheless, the reflection in the mirror is deeply hidden in the brokenness of my soul. My beloved beautiful daughters had to sip and drink from my fountain of loving them as best as I could. Just as I was angry, so are my middle and youngest daughters. At times, their resentment towards me rages in their attitudes. Rest assured, I check and correct them, never negating the truth of their reality and how they feel about or see me.

As hard as it is, I accept their truth about me at face value. Because at the end of the day, my feelings about what they say about me are the life they lived, at no fault of their own. I chose to bear them into my world of brokenness, chaos, and confusion. They didn't ask to come into this world. I brought them into it. My youngest daughter reminds me of this truth often. She also tells me, "You cannot impose your thinking or way of life upon me." She is right about this as well.

I cannot live my life for my daughters. Yet and still, the reflections in the mirror run so deep, they were imposed upon them anyway. Whatever I am not and did not know, I could not teach them. Therefore, they will have to discover, find their way, and learn on their own. The reality is that parenting doesn't come with any instruction, manuals, or directions.

We can only do the best that we can with what we are, what we have, and where we are at the moment. I encourage everyone to work on their hearts daily. Be mindful that the reflection in the mirror runs deep. As a result, I am enough of a mother for my daughters to find their own path in life by creating their own destiny, and not living my unfulfilled hopes, dreams, or aspirations. Each one of them is an unique individual outside of me.

Chapter 6

They Needed Saving from Me

I live in my truth facing the reality of my life. The reality is that I'm not perfect. Therefore, I have made some costly detrimental mistakes at the expense of my children. I don't choose to be silent or leave "this and that" in the closet. I am not too ashamed to tell that I write what I have done, been through, experienced, conquered, overcame, and been delivered from, in God's grace.

There was a time in my life when they needed saving from me. Who are "they?" My children. My beloved beautiful Sunshine, Ms. Love, and MaMa girl. I was emotionally, mentally, and physically abusive to them. I became pregnant at the age of nineteen. I didn't know who I was, and I was raging with anger and pain. I didn't love myself or even know how to do so properly. Honestly, I was depressed then. I just didn't know at that time.

So, I was numb to loving them. Although, you never saw any of my babies, youth, adolescents, teens, young women, or adults unkempt. I wasn't raised like that. I always did what I had to do. If I didn't have laundry detergent, I had a bar of bath soap or dish detergent so my babies could have clean clothes. I'd wash clothes by hand, if necessary.

I got up every morning and made breakfast for them, made sure their clothes were always pressed and ironed, and they ate and were served lunch and dinner at home on my days off. I had these tasks down. On the other hand, I didn't know how to spare the rod without going too far. No, none of my daughters ever had physical scars on them. However, the emotional and mental abuse of me calling them derogatory names had an impact and affect on them.

I used to cuss them and call them out of their names. Coming from me, their mother, was a hard pill to swallow. Here's the thing about children - they do grow up, as mine have. Now, even in the midst of my darkness, my children know I have always protected them from others. Yet, they needed saving from me. Seeing the anger they had for and towards me, I took them to counseling to tell their truth and find coping tools, skills, and resources for them to heal, blossom, and thrive into wholesome complete adults.

For me, I will never negate, downplay, or act like I didn't cause my daughters harm. Today, when you see or meet my daughters, you meet grace, poise, class, elegance, and they are respectful. In God's grace, I was an enough mother under His dominion. I know my life has been and is two-fold. Parents, don't provoke your children to wrath, and children (Colossians 3:21), children obey your parents (Ephesians 6:1). I was a whole wretch undone of a mess.

Thank God for grace and mercy, God kept my children and I because there were times in and during our lives when and where they needed saving from me. The truth shall set me free, who the Savior sets free is free indeed. The shackles of anger and pain that once held me bound have been broken. I had to own my failures, flaws, and faults to get to this place. Honesty, ownership of my wrongs, truth, and transparency on my behalf were key to our healing.

I addressed, acknowledged, and accepted their feelings and their truth without downplaying or negating their realities. My beautiful daughters and I are growing, blossoming, and thriving in a healthy loving relationship. Loving, living, and thriving in our best lives on this side of Heaven.

Born To (W)alk (i)n (N)ewness (WIN)

Chapter 7

Changing My Heart Changed My Life

The words, "Guard your heart more than anything else, because the source of your life flows from it" are those found in Proverbs 4:23 (GWT). In some versions, the word "heart" reads "thoughts." I learned in academia that one's emotions of the heart drives and fuels our behavior and actions, creating thoughts to manifest, invoking motives which affect and impact our choices.

In short, the way we feel affects the way we behave, fueling our thoughts, driving our motives. Therefore, we need to address and tend to issues of the heart in order for us to heal and become more viable productive individuals. I know I needed a heart transplant and a mind change. However, it didn't come by me doing nothing. I had to make a commitment with the intentionality that I wanted to be healed. I wanted to feel better, freed from my emotional baggage of hurt.

So, I sought counseling to talk about afflictions of my soul. Because I am open and honest with myself, I am able to address tough matters of my heart. And when the Holy Spirit, that quiet still inner voice speaks, I listen. No, I was not always where you see me today. I was extremely hypersensitive. If someone said something negative to me, I immediately wanted to respond and react. But, God sent TDJ across my path giving, sharing, and imparting wisdom and nuggets for life.

I took these gems and put them in my mental tool box, my mental psyche changing my prescriptive and the way I thought. I began to see things with a clear heart. When I became intentional, fighting through to get to the other side of breaking the cycle of loving, pursuing, and giving my time to someone who could care less about me, I was healed. It took years to break this cycle. It didn't take me overnight to get into this more than two decades of an abusive mess of a situation.

Therefore, it was not going to be an overnight process to get free from it. So, I put in the time to get better. However, it wasn't without slipping back to my old ways and habits. I just kept looking forward instead of backwards. Then, one day, the pain in my chest and heartbreak headache were gone for good. I had to hurt in order to heal. Embracing the process raw and naturally without self-medicating or masking the pain allowed me to get healed, delivered, and set free from my inner pain.

A hope and a dream wishing well will be all that we have if we don't put in the work to heal. You, I, me, us, them, and they must take ownership over matters of our hearts. We must talk about hard messy stuff in order to get and do better. Here's the thing: No one has control over our lives, except us.

Born To (W)alk (i)n (N)ewness (WIN)

Chapter 8

Encouraging Others Needing Encouragement Myself

I have been encouraging others for a very long-time while needing encouragement myself. I can remember taking a Public Speaking course in 2003 at MCCC. One of my classmates passed away, and I wrote a poem and took it to class to share with my classmates. One of my classmates said to me, "Don't give your stuff away." I have read my voice aloud and seen evidence of the gift of God's grace of encouragement upon me, with no credit or acknowledgment given.

Words of encouragement given in love and support found on obituary programs. While I have shared an abundance of words of encouragement throughout my life, with no monetary return, the blessing of the Holy Spirit's words of encouragement and affirmations have given people hope. Whatever we do in the dark with a pure and true heart, God will reward openly.

I can remember writing and sending morning inspirations in 2005. I continued doing this for some time, then I stopped. Over and throughout the course of the years, I met and sat in the company of women who I considered and took to be friends. However, some of these women stopped communicating, inviting, and taking me to their events and functions. The next thing I notice is them promoting things I introduced them to without asking me.

In 2009, I had my first gathering of women coming together in fellowship to encourage, uplift, and inspire one another to be our best selves. I would say I invited approximately twenty-five women, but only about ten showed up. I learned in that moment that it's not about the numbers, it's about impact and affect. It is about the quality and value we add, give, and bring to the lives of others.

The gift God has blessed me with has been given and shared in my identity crises, living in fornication, depression, a miscarriage, death of my baby, having to make burial arrangements for her, inadequate housing for ten years, loss of twenty years of gainful employment, suffering life changing injuries and infirmities, living in poverty, betrayal, gossip, ridicule, backbiting, and being divorced by a husband I loved dearly.

God also had me to encourage my enemies, my ex-husband's mistresses, and her child. Just as I encouraged others, I had to encourage myself, and God met me where I was. This is why I still have my sanity. This is why I praise God like I do. You know my name, you don't know my story.

Born To (W)alk (i)n (N)ewness (WIN)

Chapter 9

You Know My Name, You Don't Know My Story

There's no way you could possibly know me - I don't even know myself. I am currently fifty years old and just discovering myself through the identity and lenses of Christ. He has been revealing to me my "why" over the course of this "*Be still and know that I am God*" year. The year 2020 was a blessed year for me and my beautiful daughters. It's the year God blessed us to enter into our life of the fullness thereof.

Finally, they get a mother who is becoming wholesome. Wholesome in the sense that I am aligning with the will of Christ's heart, mind, spirit, soul, and body. I'm loving myself becoming into who Christ has chosen me to be. I no longer am *too much*. I know how to keep it classy, elegant, and simple. I am no longer over-the-top. I used to care about Jordache, Sasson, and Bujour.

These were labels, what was trending, and common. Not so much anymore. I used to iron one pants leg for half an hour. *What was wrong with me? Who does that? What a waste of time?* I no longer have time for that. But, thank you Jesus!!! Who the Savior sets free is free indeed. When God allowed me to fire myself from my job of privilege, sitting at a desk with a phone, going to work late just about everyday, prioritizing my day as I saw fit, attending to the needs of supervision without being watched or micro-managed, no one knew how to do what I did.

This was the case until I wrote and gave them a surface layout of what I did. Being a model employee going on vacation, so I thought. Then, I was deemed expendable and let go after twenty years of dedicated service. This taught me very well that I am nothing but a body to the workforce. They realized they no longer needed me, even tried to fire and blacklist me. But, I took whatever job I could get. What I do doesn't define me or make me who I am. I believe in an honest day's work for an honest day's pay, doing things in and with excellence to the best of my ability.

As a girl the age of twenty, but the inner child lost, doing adult things, not knowing what I was doing, headed for, or getting myself into, I became a broken mother. I suffered from postpartum-depression and never got treatment, counseling, or help. I would cry, feeling helpless after I gave birth to my daughter. I was disconnected and detached emotionally and mentally from my daughters for the bulk of my motherhood, until 2013. My daughters were never physically neglected, but, emotionally and mentally, I was a good enough mother. Again, you never saw any of my babies dirty, but they were neglected internally.

However, I never understood the love I see and hear when I hear other women say, "Being a mother is the best thing ever." This was not my reality emotionally or mentally. My older two daughters were not made or bore in love. They were kept because I chose not to abort the three of them, like I had done three others before them. So, when my middle daughter tells me "they were mistakes," I correct her. No, I chose to have and keep the four of you. Amirah Essence Armstrong was born and died on November 12, 2005.

She was not a stillborn. She was born extremely premature and deemed not viable medically. So, medical professionals did nothing to save her. She survived for 2hrs and 9 mins, then she passed away. I cremated her. It was a decision which haunts me until this day. For some reason, I felt she was too small to be buried in the Earth. She is an angel urn, who I need to put in a final resting place.

However, at the time of her passing, I didn't have the finances to do so. Yet, looking back, I probably could have done something better if I had been in my right mind. The Lord has had mercy on me. After all that I endured, experienced and been through in my life, I still have a sense of mental well-being. So, I am immensely beyond thankful and grateful to God for how He's kept me through it all.

The most challenging part of my life's journey has been that I have always had to make it alone. I didn't have much support along the way. But from a toddler, youth, and into an adult, I found my way as best as I could. I can't lie, it hurts sometimes not having anyone to call in times of need. No one to depend on. Thankfully, I pray reaching into my God-given soul of resilience, tenacity, and strength saying, "In the name of Jesus, you can do all things through Christ who strengthens you." And, so can you.

Although I stumble and have fallen along the way, God has picked me up according to His word, if a righteous man falls seven times, he gets up every time (Proverbs 24:16). I am living and seeking the kingdom of righteousness. Here, everything is added unto us. You know my name, you don't know my story. So, be mindful of self, loved ones, friends, and enemies, and don't judge others. Lest you forget, you too have a story.

Chapter 10

Accepting Being Set Apart

Looking at the title of this chapter from a 50-year-old perspective is a gift and a blessing. On the other hand, looking at it through the lense of a lonely child who feels abandoned, isolated and alone, these words take on a different meaning. I am not worthy, accepted, or good enough to belong to or be a part of the group. In turn, this could leave one feeling like an unwanted outcast in a culture that thrives on the sense that being popular is "*in*," *hip*, and *live*.

In reality, going against the grain is more appealing. However, one must have tough skin to stand alone in truth and honesty by being true to self. Feelings of rejection and dejection will later be our saving grace of character enhancement. Being in a volatile, hostile environment where those in authority know your stance is a blessing for elevation. Becoming abnormal when order is not followed according to policies, procedures, or protocol makes you an elite asset.

In life, there is no *get in where we fit in*. We <u>must</u> be willing to go the distance of the journey, finding our way to make a way, not getting stuck or stagnant in the obstacles or challenges we will face and endure. Therefore, it is always imperative to encourage yourself with the words "I can, I shall, I will find the strength and courage to get up again after a fall."

Never discard or discount authentic genuine love, support, or correction for the better of your greater good. To whom much is given, much is also required. You have been set apart to be great. Never settle for being less by being and doing mediocre or mundane by the company you keep. Choose your surroundings well.

Chapter 11

Unique Individual

There will come a time in life where and when we must lay aside every distraction which hinders us from living a good life on purpose. However, for some of us, there may be hidden pain causing us to be stuck in the existence of where we are. In life, there is no one size fits all. Therefore, we can tailor and write our ending as we see fit. No, we don't have to take no for an answer, however, we must go our separate ways by knocking on doors to find our yes.

This requires having and setting a standard of excellence for oneself, accompanied with an honorable character. There is never *getting in where you fit in*. Instead, we must learn to be set apart from the rest. Walking in our own brand of excellence by knowing where we are is not our last destination or final stop. Before we get to where we want and desire to be, we must operate like we are already there.

I embody an attitude of gratitude and a standard of excellence.

Every deed I do is not unto man, instead, I am serving and working as unto the Lord. He is my source resource and way maker. When I had nothing, He supplied all my needs according to His riches and glory. I went through some things, they made me better. But, there were many tears shed along the way which make me the unique individual I am. My shoes are custom and tailor made. There is no other pair like them. They are one of a kind, as are yours.

So, never get caught up in fitting in with what is popular. Especially, when you are calling yourself abnormal. Being abnormal means operating and going against the grain. Making your own lane and staying grounded and rooted in humility and integrity. Set apartness will require you to know that you are a unique individual. Therefore, you will never be able to do what the Roman's do. Thus, repent, change your thinking and change your life.

When you have been chosen, you cannot move like everyone else. Embrace being an unique individual by always moving in and with righteousness. All else will fail. Living in righteousness is fail-proof.

Chapter 12

Footprints to finding my Identity

The cards of life dealt me were a jaded, twisted, premonition of who I was. The world told me that I was dark, ugly, unwanted, not worthy, nor valued. I didn't, couldn't, and wouldn't amount to anything. No one would listen or pay attention to what I had to bring or add to the quality of life amounting to anything, or give me recognition for my accomplishments.

Broken relationships bridged with boys, males, and men took an essence of my worth that I will never get back. I wasn't a paid sex worker or a prostitute but, I was giving myself away in search of the person I knew I could be. My fathers loving me as best as he knew how, along with shattered innocence stolen never given atonement or reparation broke my spirit.

All I ever wanted was for these boys, males, and men to say, "I was wrong for abusing, using, misusing, and hurting you. Please forgive me." Only two out of many were mature enough to make the hurt of their pain inflicted upon me righteous.

Nonetheless, the wheels of life keep on turning. I had to find a way to get my healing finding my identity in who Christ says I am. Here, never again, will I ever be looking or thirsting for love in all the wrong places while being dehydrated by people who are so quick to judge the work, actions, and pain of another.

We never know the story of a person's identity, or the place where we encounter, meet, and see them currently. If we can't say anything nice, say a prayer. We all have flaws, skeletons, and chinx in our closets. So, have some empathy and compassion toward one another.

Ask yourself, "What are my footprints? What are the cards life dealt me? What cards am I currently holding in my hands today?" Must we never forget the cards of life can change in a blink of an eye. Note to Self: Lord, help me to always remember my struggles.

Chapter 13

Mother under God's Dominion

No one gets to choose our race, color, or creed. They are given and assigned to us by an authority higher than ourselves. The society we are born into has placed stipulations needing and requiring reformation upon me long before I was born. I wasn't given equal opportunities, nor was I afforded the same privileges as my white peers. This is a history fact and truth nugget of my reality.

White privilege has afforded a platform title '16 and Pregnant' for predominantly-white teens giving them leverage and a platform to financial wealth and stability. While someone who looks like me is labeled as a "Black unwed mother." As I saw this time and time again, I began to realize life and death is in the power of the tongue. I am a mother under God's dominion. The act of fornication is the actual sin, not my children. For this reason, repentance of sin removes and erases the guilt that goes along with it.

Therefore, we must always do our willed best to reach in our internal self by speaking life over ourselves. The life I live in public is the praise of my private worship and thanksgiving. My children have had to live in the privacy of my brokenness and abuse. I was emotionally, mentally, and physically abusive to them. I have never left physical scars on them. However, the middle and youngest experienced hurt, pain, wounds, and affliction to come out in their communication projected towards and at me.

I take, receive, and accept their truth and reality because it is their truth, and I must respect it. I cannot and will not negate the truth of their reality to save face for myself. I am a mother under God's dominion and grace. My ministry starts in the walls of my home. There is no way I will live a life with the world praising me while my daughters have great resentment, animosity, and disdain towards me.

This is not the life I want for me or them. I birthed them into my pain of not knowing how to love myself or knowing my identity. From the beginning of my motherhood, up until the age of forty-eight years old, I was still a broken,cussing, and fussing mother. With each passing day, I work to strive to be a more loving, wiser, kinder, better, stronger me. I am a mother under God's dominion.

Chapter 14

Not About that Life

None of my children's fathers can ever say I caused them anxiety, headaches, or ill intent. I was a lost and confused woman who put my big girl panties on and took care of their daughters in their absence. The one thing I did preach, ask, and request is for them to be a present first man in their lives so they wouldn't suffer from 'Broken Ideology of a Man' syndrome like me. Chasing, looking for, longing for the love and protection of a man a father sets the tone in our formative years. Oh, my unaware bossy vocal self checked them on this - more so the first and the last of the three.

My middle daughter's father never needed me to tell him what a man is or does. The way he treated me was due to the depths of brokenness in his "manality" and mentality. But, he always showed up as a father to her all but once, to get at me. Thankfully, she was too young to remember. However, my mother and I surely never forgot.

Nevertheless, he has made recompense and reparations for the error of his ways. He is very supportive and encourages me to be my best self. I forgave him for the remnants his pain inflicted upon me while he was in the darkness of his pain. On the other hand, just as my own father, my first and last daughter's fathers love them the best they know how.

My oldest daughter's father is the most meek out of the three. She has his gentle, caring, compassionate, spirit. He could have been my husband had I been aware of my identity. But, like I said, in the chapter, 'It Wasn't the Marriage to Him, It Was Me,' I had deep-rooted pain that I was unaware of. I wasn't good for myself, let alone anyone else.

Then, to end up bridging lifelong relationships with men who have characteristics and traits of my father. This curse of mine has to be broken with me never again to arise again. I declare and decree this for my daughters, in the name of Jesus. Broken toxic relationships of dysfunction die and end with me. I never was nor will I ever be about bashing my daughter's fathers to them. To me, this is beyond wrong!!! I laid with these men and conceived them.

Whatever issues, dislikes, disdain, or concerns I have about or with them are mine, not theirs. I am not about that life. Each of my children's fathers have their truths, convictions, and reservations about which I will not dispute or refute, because it is their truth. What I do know is that I and they know I would have never gone to child support out of spite. I have gone without for my children. As long as I have breath in my body as their mother, I have been and will always be there for mine. On the other hand, I never will be about the life of tearing a man down. There's no need because his character and integrity speaks volume for themselves.

Thankfully, my daughters are able to make their own conscious, unbiased judgment concerning and regarding their relationships with their fathers without any negative character- bashing from me about them. As stated before, I have never been about that life, nor will I ever be.

Born To (W)alk (i)n (N)ewness (WIN)

Chapter 15

Pushing Thru Darkness into the Light

The world has been pressing down on me long before I could remember. It seems as if my existence was one which the world sought to abort. It robbed me of my identity way before I had the chance to come into myself. My steps have been shaky and unsteady all of my life. I learned early on if I wanted something in life, I had to knock down doors going to seek my blessings.

Best believe, when Bronda Bessant pulls up and comes through, excellence comes with me. Even in my flaws falling down, I'm through with everything I have by giving you the best version of me in the moment. So many seconds, minutes, hours, days, weeks, months, and years I sat in darkness longing for someone to listen, someone to communicate with, and someone to at least try to understand to hear my pain crying out loudly from the pit of my soul. But, no one was ever there.

So, I went numb, going into myself like a turtle putting its body into its shell. There I stayed sleeping my life away. At times, I didn't eat for days on end. I didn't have an appetite due to my mental state at the time. My body didn't register to my brain that I was hungry. I had emotionally, mentally, and spiritually tapped out of life. I was in such a deep dark place of confusion and lost, wondering how I kept ending up in the vicious cycle of being a single mother trying to do it all on my own. I cried, I cried, and I cried. Weep, weep, weeping my way to morning.

With each passing day, my infants grew from babies to toddlers, from toddlers to youth, from youth to adolescents, from adolescents to pre-teens, to young adults, and two are now grown. One more to go. It was a rough journey, thankfully after many, many years spent pushing through the darkness, I finally made it into the light. However, it wasn't without a battle.

I had to fight declaring, decreeing, and proclaiming my way to sanity. I told the devil many many days, "You can't and won't take my mind." The prayers of my praying mother have kept me. And here I am today, better than I have ever been. Forging ahead to what God has for me. I count it all joy knowing that I am truly blessed. Never give up on God, because He won't give up on you.

Chapter 16

My Love Has Conditions

Unconditional love of loving myself begins with me. No longer will I entertain, accept, or place myself in a position where love is not being served and administered. As a woman of self-love, value, worth, respect, assurance, integrity, kindness, authenticity, and dignity, no man will get my time if he is not self-aware and whole to himself.

I will love, support, and come alongside the right man who knows his identity, self-value, and worth. I will not stand for anyone trying or coming to take or chip away at my self-esteem or confidence. A relationship is not work, its love must be maintenanced and nurtured in order to keep its strength, tenacity, and fortitude. I am no longer giving away my priceless gifts for free.

I don't need money. I need love, a pure heart with no motives or hidden agendas, a character of moral excellence, honesty, integrity, truthfulness, respect, and "your word is your bond" actions to align type of love. I need the love that I am a gift to be honored, appreciated, and reciprocated in equal diligence.

I now know whatever a man needs and wants in his life, he will do nothing to hurt in any shape, form, or fashion. He will provide, protect, and go to war for me. The kind of Babyface love found in *'As Soon as I Get Home.'* Any sign of disrespect, you gotta go! 'Cause at fifty, loving myself and being confident in and with 'MY' value and worth, I ain't beat for the unware man games of child's play love of disrespect!

I will have a love where the man loves me as Christ loves the church. Not looking or waiting on it - I got to be about my Father's business serving others. So, I am going to continue my work of loving others as Christ has loved me. This entails encouraging, uplifting, and inspiring others to aspire to be their best selves by helping when I can and am assigned to assisting each and everyone.

Those God chooses to send to understanding they too are born to walk in newness. My love has conditions, and so should yours. If someone leaves, let them go. If someone one walks away, let them go. Not loving ourselves causes the pain of death to die. Love must have conditions. If not, rest assured it will be abused, devalued, and unappreciated in selfish unaware hands. Be mindful of who you give the love of your heart to. Giving it, putting it, and entrusting it to an unaware, broken, individual it is surely to be abused, misused, and broken.

Therefore, please don't make the mistake I did for so very long. My love now has conditions. Thank you, Jesus my soul is now like Raid to roaches. Anyone who is not righteous doesn't get too close. Loving and forgiving self are two priceless gifts to be treasured. Keep them close.

Born To (W)alk (i)n (N)ewness (WIN)

Chapter 17

A Long Road to Finding a Place to Call Home

As I have referenced in several of my other writings, my daughters and I lived in my mother's one bedroom apartment for the past ten years. During the course of this time, I lost sustainable employment and wages of twenty years. I lived off unemployment of $400 a week, grossing $18,000 in 2018, and experienced relinquished child support arrears valued at more than $65,000.

I went 'THRU' some things. Thankfully, by God's grace, I'm wiser and stronger than I've ever been. In our time of transition, my middle daughter was blessed to go away to college coming out with only $1,600 in loans, after a $250,000 education. I wish this was *my* story. Nevertheless, I completed my Associate's Degree in 2013 that

Born To (W)alk (i)n (N)ewness (WIN)

I started in 2003.

Then, I went on to get my Bachelor's in 2016 in Biblical Studies, go figure. This wasn't my choice. However, the program I enrolled in offered this as a continuation of transitioning from an Associate's Degree, to a Bachelor's. I have been writing and sharing the gospel with others daily off-and-on since 2005. Now, looking back, I see God was equipping me to be able to rightfully share His word with others for interpretation, implication, and application for our lives. This was not my doing or desire. It is God's purposed will and plan for my life.

In 2017, I began pursuing my Master's Degree. It's currently on hold until I get directions and instructions from Christ on where, when, and how to complete this part of my journey. I prayed and shed a lot of tears along the way. Crying, cussing, and screaming - but I never gave up. What I am most grateful and thankful for are my mother's love for me and my girls. I know we got on her last nerve something awful most of the time, but she never said a negative word. She's an epitome of what it is to be a Proverbs 31 woman.

I'm grateful to call her mother. During my search to find a place to call home, it was overwhelming to say the least. So much has changed from 1998, when I last looked for a place. To complicate my search even more, I was attempting to work with a 503C agency to assist with my security deposit. In addition to the security deposit, they were going to provide me with assistance, paying three to six months in rent.

The stipulations of the program were stringent. Not to mention, most landlords were not willing to have a third party involved. So, I prayed, stepping out on faith. As I type this message, I still have a few more matters to complete in order to secure the lease. Truly, I'm prayerful that God has ordained and orchestrated my steps. Working with an agency to find housing is something I am very unfamiliar with, since I have always found a way to make a way. And oftentimes, when I sought help, it felt very condescending.

What I mean by this is, the representative for the agency from which I was seeking help seemed a bit judgmental to me. It was as if I was looking for a *handout*, instead of a helping hand. I am not one who sits around plotting, searching, and seeking how I can get over on or play the system. I have always worked for everything I have. So, to find myself in such an overwhelming delicate situation in my life was already hard enough. Then, to add insult to injury, I have to endure feeling scrutinized in order to get assistance. It seems as if the system is set up for failure for someone who looks like me.

Nevertheless, God provided me with the strength to endure, stand, and preserve. While working with the agency, my case manager was very warm and welcoming. However, she would send me to look at places located in areas that did not meet the criteria of what I was looking for. I informed her during my intake that I worked nights and needed to be somewhere which felt safe enough when I left and returned home from work. She sent me to neighborhoods where there had been recent shootings where someone was killed. Or, the environment was not friendly for my lifestyle. Then, I met the director and he seemed cold and nonchalant to my needs.

In addition to my experience, the agency required me to be committed to get counseling for managing my life, which was not something I needed. I very well understood I had to pay my bills for where I live. I shared with them that I have always been gainfully employed up until 2013, when I was led on from twenty years of dedicated service.

In my time since then, I have always worked for whatever company who called and offered me a job. I never looked at what I did in the past, which was sit at a desk with a phone doing clerical work. I worked in a freezer for 10-12 hours a day or beyond. I worked 10-11 hour shifts, standing on my feet the entire time making the best of the blessings God had given me.

So, to come to a place in my life where I had to endure having to feel as if I was less than a person felt demoralizing to me. I talked to my friend, LA. She advised me to take the money for the downpayment and whatever assistance the agency was offering so that I could hold onto the money I saved up. But, my time at the hotel was coming to an end. There were no more resources left to pay for my room.

Therefore, I sought out housing from earlier June until I found a place to stay. I met with several realtors who were supposed to be assisting me. However, the first two were not very helpful. Me being ignorant to the process of working with a real estate agent did not know my respective agent should have accompanied me to every property I viewed as well as contact the listing agent if it was not their property, and go with me to view it. Well, this was not my experience and I was not aware.

My initial and second agent had no intention of assisting me in securing a home. Neither of them walked me through the properties, or had any listing information to give about the properties. But, one of them googled me and viewed my LinkedIn page. It was as if she did not feel I could afford the place I was looking at. Furthermore, the environment did not feel welcoming to me or my children. So, we kept looking.

When we arrived at the place God blessed us to settle in, we met and encountered an agent of Asian descent. When I tell you he has been honest, helpful, warm, and welcoming. He has been honest, helpful, warm, and welcoming. Upon meeting him, I informed him I was already working with an agent. He asked, "Where is your agent? Whoever they are, they know they were supposed to come with you." He also said, "This would be a waste of my time. Who is going to get the commission?"

He explained the entire process and steps to working with an agent and securing a home. In addition to this, he greeted us with his name, addressing my daughter and I by our names from the very beginning. He had all the information on the property listing, in conjunction with giving us his employment history. As a result of me finding my own place and paying for my down payment, I was disqualified from the program that was supposed to assist me in finding a home. Thus, I know wherever there are people, there will be out of orderliness sometimes. For the most part, the place God blessed us with as a home is in an environment that feels safe and is family-friendly.

It's very peaceful, in the cut, out of the way, very close to our lifestyle and entertainment needs. It is also close to the interstate in order to get to work, with several accessible ways, in case of detours or road construction. I don't have many whom I consider friends. Therefore, I won't be having much company. In addition to this, the COVID pandemic restrictions have me leery of refuting breaking protocol running the risk of getting infected with the virus.

I know I can't afford to or want to get any sicker than I already am - let alone run the risk of exposing others in my condition and state. So, I refrain from entertaining others in my home. Nonetheless, two of my longtime family childhood friends of more than thirty-five years came to check on me to make sure I was really doing okay.

LT, was my maid of honor in my wedding. She should have been all my daughter's Godmother as well. I trust her to make sure my babies (now ladies) are okay. She and her husband come from Philadelphia, PA to see me. She blessed us with the gifts of necessity to living by the way of providing us with dishes, glasses, pots, and pans.

HG, called one day saying, "I'm in the area. Can I stop by to see you?" He was in town conducting business, coming to Jersey from Delaware. When he arrived, I told him to park in my spot. He pulled up in a Tesla. This was a vision and reminder of the place God blessed me to call home was a blessed place. See, both of these individuals who came to see me, are my witnesses and can affirm my story because they also came to see me in rehab.

I was embarrassed when LT came to visit when I was at my mother's, due to having no comfortable place to entertain her, because the living room, me and daughters bedroom were all we had at the time, living in my mother's one bedroom apartment, and having one bathroom. Now, ten years later, they came to visit me in my own home for the time with two bathrooms, and a laundry room, in a private community. To God be the glory! TDJ mentioned in *Watch Who You Undress Before*, can also voche for my truth, as he knows my name, not my story.

He too has been in the presence of my God-anointed, appointed, assigned blessed home for the time being. My immediate family knows my journey and story to finding a home along with my friend and confidant EW who passed away in May 2019. I sent LA pictures of my walk-in, but she has not yet been to my home. But, she too has been in the parking lot of my mother's complex. So, she can also affirm the validity of my walk of faith and my journey to finding a place to call home.

It has been a long fifteen years to finally find love, joy, and peace resting in the arms of Jesus. This part of my journey didn't conclude with my husband being sent at this time. Yet, I am blessed all the same. My relationship with my Lord and Savior, healer, deliverer, comforter, keeper, provider, sustained, my EVERYTHING I need Him to be when I need Him is at the pinnacle of getting stronger, greater, and better.

I wouldn't change a thing about my life's journey - God has blessed me every step of the way. It's been a long journey to finding a home. Now, I have been blessed with this temporary safe haven, and I'm working towards remaining emotionally, mentally and physically healthy because I know greater is coming. In the meantime, I am basking in the blessing of my daughters and I having our own home. It's been a long journey to finding a place to call home. I live in Canaan. My name is victory. I have survived and am thriving in Jesus's love, grace, and mercy.

Because He's no respective person, what He has done for me, my daughters, and so many others, He will do for you. I pray reading my story gives you hope to never quit or give up hope no matter how dark or hopeless your life, world, state, or condition may seem. Love, prayers, hugs, joy, peace, and blessings abound you always. Never give up on yourself or lose hope. God has a blessing with your name on the other side of your pain. I'm a living witness with the testimony you're reading, 'Born to (W)alk (i)n (N)ewness (WIN).

Born To (W)alk (i)n (N)ewness (WIN)

Chapter 18

Cut from a Different Cloth

Lord knows I cannot, will not, and am not speaking for anyone else. I don't know what you are dealing with, or have dealt with in the compounds of the walls of your home. But, I have and am living a life with my children where each of us are evolving and arising through, and beyond the ashes of brokenness; growing, becoming the best versions of ourselves.

And, this isn't void of going and growing through our own emotional pain. For me, what I have found to be true with myself and my youngest two daughters is that you cannot tell a wayward child to grow anything and they receive it openly, at least from me. These two youngest children of mine will not accept, receive, or hear any gentle suggestions of love coming from me. Instead, they will eat from my acclaim and accolades.

What are my acclaim and accolades? The sweat of my brow off my back. In layman's terms, benefiting from the fruits of my labor. It seems as if they feel entitled to my blessings. Now, you already read, 'A Long Journey to Finding a Home.' It **was** a long journey to finding a home!!! Now, whatever my mother did for me growing, in between, up until now, I am beyond grateful and thankful for. Even in my lost, wandering, messed up, lost and confused state, I always served my mother well.

This morning as I type this, I am in a medical physical crisis, and I have been going through health and medical issues of some sort since March 22, 2020 when I was exposed to COVID in the line of duty at work. As I wrote in one of my earlier reflections, I was punched in the face on January 28, 2021 at my job. While I saw this unfortunate turn of circumstances as an unwanted dilemma, it has also been a blessing in disguise. A blessing with a new pain and prayer of concern.

I received a concussion and neck strain. As a result, I have been sidelined initially out of commission for the first four weeks. During this time, I didn't drive and only went out to go to doctor's appointments. For the first time ever, as a mother, I sat still. I was sitting all the way down. This pandemic showed me and my two entitled daughters they could make it on their own without me, while loving, supporting and helping one another.

The doctor has me on strict restrictions. I am limited and restricted to what I can physically do. For me, this is okay because my health is my wealth. My neck isn't in good shape, according to medical professionals. They are recommending cortisone shots in my neck. *No, thank you doctor for your expertise.* I'm not a proponent or a fan of taking shots or getting any surgery on my neck.

Therefore, I will take the recommended medications and go to physical therapy to condition my muscles for strength, fortitude, and endurance for my healing. I told my middle daughter the doctor said, "No intimate contact." I didn't get what he was saying at the time. However, as I was talking to her on our trip to the grocery store to get her a ham, it registered. No, sexual activities.

Well, that's easy to manage. I have been out of commission since 2017. I'm good with it. My last soul tie smash, wake up, self-love, worth, and value reality-check was with someone else's husband at the time. Never again. I got him while still married to me, accepted him in my own pain. My daughters knew the pain I was in. They have been with me this entire journey from my lowest state of brokenness to my wholesomely blessed now.

They know they never saw their mother physically down and out-of-commission. I am one to make things happen and get things done. If you don't come see me or check on me, I will pray, put my faith to work, willing myself to tap into my inner strength, and put it with the power of God's might doing the best I can with what strength I have. I don't lay down accepting defeat.

This isn't who God made me. Oh, rest assured, my daughters know!!! So, please help me understand why these blessed children of mine feel they can have me as mama the do-it-all maid, at their service beck and call. I realized they are just like how my siblings and I were. My mother pampered us!! And I too have pampered them in a sense by giving them more than I had growing up.

My mother has blessed my children and I with a hedge of protection. I cannot thank God or her enough for how they have favored us. This is why for the life of me, I don't understand or cannot comprehend where their lack of zest and zeal is seeing and reaching within themselves where their greatness comes from. Meaning taking and receiving every opportunity as growth instead of nonchalant, mediocre, or mundane.

This reminds me never to compare my children to myself or each other, but to love, embrace, and accept them for who they are and where they are. While I am driven, ambitious, goal-oriented, introverted, outcoming to get everything God has for me, knocking on doors, taking whatever opportunity comes my way, seeing no task or job as beneath me. I must also accept that my children are of a new generation and are cut from a different cloth also.

If they choose not to put in the necessary effort and work to make something happen for themselves, it's not my fault. They are who they are. And I am who I am. We are all cut from a different cloth. No two individuals are the same. Own your own lane and write of passage, writing the vision to your own destiny, at your pace. As long as you have life, health, and strength, it's never too late to live a life knowing you are Born to (W)alk (i)n (N)ewness (WIN).

Born To (W)alk (i)n (N)ewness (WIN)

Chapter 19

To My Black Man

I am your Black queen, your rib, prayer partner, lover of your soul having your at best interest at heart, in the will of Christ's perfect will for your life. I am deeply concerned about and for you and your well-being. I am a beautiful, dark-skinned woman, wrapped in the beautiful skin God gave me. He knew I could handle your ostracization of not being good enough, unwanted, too much, rejected, and not worthy of love or to be loved. I am praying for you.

As strong as I am, I was created to look to you for direction and instruction, as you are called and meant to be the head, and not the tail. However, as intelligent as you are, you have lost your way. You condescend me when I seek your wisdom. You take shots throwing darts at my character. Nope, you know I checked you on that. My question to you is, what happened with or to the love of your mother, your first Lady? How are you loving? Do you or did you even love her? At this point, you stay in your feelings. You are more emotionally charged than I am. I know, I wear the chinks of my armor on my sleeves.

My vulnerability, my weakness to let you know you are safe with me. I will cover your heart. On the other hand, you are sure enough going to be the best man you are purposed to be. 'Cause, I am always praying with and for you, when you can't or don't know to pray for yourself.

However, I must admit, I was a bit taken aback by your lack of awareness of who you are. You should rejoice with me in my blessings of grace and mercy, during and in my seasons of trials and tribulations. Instead, you cut me down when you can visually and physically see that I am weak, and need your love and support. But, I could be broken, fragmented, and shattered if I didn't know who and whose I am. You need not assist me when I need you.

No worries, I charge it to your head and not your heart. When you really sit still embracing the moment, the error of your ways will come to remembrance. And when it does, rewind and apologize for the offenses sowed while coming into yourself. Thankfully, I am in a place where Christ has healed me. Therefore, I can extend you the same grace extended He to me. Please make no mistake, you will never have or be given a pass to disrespect me. You have been checked and warned. I love, adore, admire, honor, and respect you.

In return, I need the same from, and of, you. Love, prayers, hugs, and blessings abound always.

Born To (W)alk (i)n (N)ewness (WIN)

Chapter 20

Don't Chase After a Man

"Find a good spouse, you find a good life— and even more: the favor of God!" Proverbs 18:22, MSG

Daughter, life lessons don't come easy. Sometimes, they come by way of life experiences becoming life skills. When I speak to you, I come in the name of love, not harm or judgment. I just don't want you to walk the same path I took. Daddy issues of not having an awareness of a loving father leaves evidence of devoid self-value and worth. Not knowing how a man is supposed to love you, which causes you to wind up abusing yourself by chasing after a man, is something girls or women should never do.

Trust me, I get it. Been there, done it, so I know what I am talking about. Calling unlimited, texting, and straight crowding the man's space when it is evident he is not interested. He was ghosting, not answering the phone, or responding to text messages. On the other hand, here you are jumping at his every text prompt, responding to favors asking to max out your bank account, borrowing funds, burning gas, and bucking up the mileage on your dash. During the process, warnings come one after the other.

You stay out in the streets all times of night, lying about your deeds, while your physical appearance and vehicle looks like all hell. Daughter, you better wake up before it is too late. You have been warned that women don't chase after a man. Mommy is talking and speaking from current experience of embracing and coming into her self-value and worth. A man needs or requires nothing from a woman, other than for her to be good.

This is in the terms of our possessions of our physical, emotional, and mental well-being. Most definitely, he does not want or require our tangible resources. A man is good when his woman and family are loved, protected, and provided for. My life's lessons taught me beyond well: Don't pursue or chase after a man.

Chapter 21

I Don't Care What People Say

Lord knows, I don't write just to write. What you are reading was written by me by way of and through the Holy Spirit. As I am writing, the words are just flowing and coming to me. It's 12:16 AM now. Oftentimes, I write in the wee hours of the morning when I should be sleeping. Whenever God lays it on my heart to send a message of encouragement to somebody, I send it in obedience.

Life is not written and doesn't come with instructions without knowledge. In order to live a righteous life, I had to put away my childish ways (1 Corinthians 13:11), pick up my cross, and follow Jesus (Luke 9:23). Every saint has a past and every sinner has a future. I don't care what people say about me. God knows my truth, life, and abilities. Where it is an offense on my behalf, I will turn around, go back, and make it right. After that, it's no longer on me.

I'm moving forward in and with the life Christ has purposed for me. I'm not going to allow anyone or anything to break me. You can talk, gossip, and backbite all you like. You ain't nothing but a rock-thrower. Please be very mindful that while you are throwing rocks, none of us live in glass houses. While you are busy pointing fingers of judgment, rest assured you have a rock with your name on it. I don't care how pure we think, believe, feel, and self-righteous we are, we are all as filthy rags in the sight of Jesus (Isaiah 64:6).

So, you just go ahead with your backbiting, unwanted thoughts, schemes, and lies because any hole you attempt to dig for me or anyone else for that matter is going to be your own. Be assured that sowing and reaping is real. You're gonna reap what you sow. You better pray God's hand doesn't pass you and land on your loved ones for your deeds committed and done in secret, in conjunction with your blatant disrespect.

Please don't worry about me or mine, I am giving you a glimpse of my truth, my reality, the life I have lived, triumphed, and persevered through and beyond. Judge, condemn, backbite, throw rocks, lie, and hate all you like. My skin is thick and tough now, and I don't care what people say. You don't have a Heaven or Hell to put me in. No matter how much I stumble, stagger, or fall, I will arise still being God's child. And He loves me, I, you, we, us, them, and they in spite of us.

So, love yourself much, forgive yourself, and others even more. And live a good life in and of purpose.

Born To (W)alk (i)n (N)ewness (WIN)

Chapter 22

This is Who God Made Me

No one to call, depend, or count on. I am there for everyone else. But, when I need and call for assistance, no one is there for me, even if they say, "Call me if you need something." Then, I feel like I can depend on or call on my sister. Wrong answer. I am always met with a pause of silence. Oh, let me let my supervisor know. Me, thinking after I hung up, *I don't like grudgingly givers*. Lord, help me in meeting this need request.

I called my Sunshine, my oldest daughter and I asked her. Her response was, "Okay, Mom." I told my middle daughter about my dilemma. She just got a driver's permit. Even with anxiety about driving, she said, "Mom, I can drive you." I am so thankful for my selfless ladies. We are a team. We have our differences, but when the rubber meets the road, we are there to support one another. On the other hand, I realize people can only give us what they have within themselves.

What I have found to be true for me is, God has equipped me with a tenacity of resilience and perseverance. Most days, for the past year and eight days now have been lonely, trying days for me. But, my sister did pop up a couple of times without being asked. I was beyond thankful for the gesture of love and kindness.

However, this does not relegate the fact I feel her personality traits towards me is not one of service. Her hurtful behavior saddens me to the point of cutting her off. I am beyond tired of the strained relationship that is an ebb and flow of unhealthy pace for me. Therefore, I am bowing out gracefully from people whom I keep telling your actions towards me are hurting me. So, I must make the choice to do what's best for me. I digress, and bow out gracefully. I will not be a victim. Thank you for listening too and allowing me to vent.

This was chronicled in the heat of my feelings. My younger self was not so loving, kind, or nice to my sister. As a result, as much as she loves me, our relationship had been fractured. Being the person I am, believes ministry begins at home. So, I have made atonement for any and all harm that my unaware, ignorant, selfish, lost self caused my loved ones. I now live in love, joy, and peace with my family these days. I went to them asking for forgiveness in and with the action and heart of love. The old me has died. I am now living the life of knowing I am Born to (W)alk (i)n (N)ewness(WIN).

In Concluding................

Never allow the cards you are dealt in life cripple, hinder, or stop you from becoming who you are purposed and destined to be. For sure, life is hard, not easy, just, or fair. It's not for the faint or weak. It will swallow us up whole without remorse. Therefore, when we are old enough, we must find the inner strength to get up, stand up, and say, "No more."

My no more was healing from existing in anger, hurting in pain, giving myself away to the most deadliest sin of fornication. Birthing children out of wedlock, suffering depression, being homeless, having a miscarriage, experiencing poverty, and being divorced by a husband I loved dearly. I refuse to be a victim to the cards life dealt me. I prayed, I had faith, and put in the work to my healing. I got up knowing I was Born to (W)alk (i)n (N)ewness (WIN).

Being Born to (WIN) is subjective. Meaning, it will mean something different to each one of us. Nonetheless, it is possible to and for you. It's possible you're holding my testimony in your hands. The questions are: How bad do you want it? *"It"* means your healing. Getting up is not easy. How are you planning on intentionally investing in your healing? What actions and steps are you going to take here?

Born To (W)alk (i)n (N)ewness (WIN)

ABOUT THE AUTHOR

I, Bronda Bessant, am now a fifty-year-old woman who has confronted, addressed, and attended to the cry of my inner child's afflictions finding healing in my identity of who Christ says I am. God is healing, mending, and growing the relationship of my daughters daily. Each one of us is growing into our healthy, wholesome, best selves. However, we each have some scars, scratches, and bruises, which require intentional attending to, in order to keep growing, gleaning, and glistening in all that is purposed for our lives.

I have been employed in the warehouse industry for more than twenty-four years while serving and seeking justice for myself and others. Then, in 2018, God chose me to serve the The New Jersey Department of Health as a MSO. It is here along with my academic knowledge where I discovered I was my first patient, consumer, inmate, family, friend, and loved one. I was put in a place where life could have been very well taken, or I ended being. Reality really shook me to the core.

TDJ often asked me what detail I liked best. My answer was, "I like them all." In a sense, I am thankful to have sustainable gainful employment, after my training for reigning from 2013-2018, when I had to accept whatever job I could get. I went from working 8.2 hours a day to 10-12 hours, going home when the work was done by shifts daily. I dare not complain. Not me! I won't. I know my story, you only know my name.

In this book, you read the naked, honest, pure, and real occurrences of my life's journey. My footprints are not pretty. But, I wouldn't trade my shoes with anyone, as they are custom tailor-made. There's no other pair like them. Keep believing you too can (W)alk (i)n (N)ewness (WIN).

www.ingramcontent.com/pod-product-compliance
Lightning Source LLC
Chambersburg PA
CBHW021430070526
44577CB00001B/140